I Got Married
if you can believe that

Other Books by Jim

I Went to College and it was okay
I Got a Job and it wasn't that bad
I Made Some Brownies and they were pretty good

I Got Married
if you can believe that

by Jim

Andrews and McMeel
A Universal Press Syndicate Company
Kansas City

Today I got home from the copy store around 4 p.m.

I was really tired, so I took a nap.

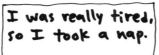

When I got up it was 6 o'clock.

For a second, I couldn't tell if it was morning or night.

Today Steve came over and said, "I'm bored."

We sat around for a while.

"I'm still bored," Steve said.

Today at the copy store I made copies while Julie worked the register.

Somebody came in and asked us to copy a magazine article he clipped out.

Julie said we can't copy it because of copyright laws and everything, which is store policy.

The guy just stood there for a while then Julie took the article and said, "Aw, heck, we'll copy it."

Today Ruth and I ate at a nice restaurant.

The waiter brought us some water and said he'd be right back.

He didn't come back for quite a while and Ruth said, "I wonder if he forgot about us."

But he eventually came and took our order.

Today Steve told me he really wanted a plant.

"I think it would brighten up my life considerably." he said.

So I told him he should probably go buy one.

But he said he didn't feel like getting up.

I decided to start reading a book today because I was bored.

The other day Steve loaned me a copy of watership Down and said I should read it.

As I started reading, I noticed the glue on the binding was kind of old.

Then I noticed I could pull out all the pages with no effort.

Steve and I went to a greenhouse today.

They had hundreds of different kinds of plants, and we'd never even heard of most of them.

Steve really liked this one tree-type thing, but it was 350 dollars, not including the pot.

"You could buy a whole forest for that," he said.

Today Ruth and I went for a walk.

We passed by a cat in front of a house.

Ruth stopped to pet him and said, "Hi fella," and he seemed friendly.

I leaned down to pet him and he took off running, and Ruth said, "You scared him off, Jim!"

Today at the copy store Julie, Joel, Dan and I took our break at the same time.

We were all talking when Julie started telling a story about washing her smock.

Halfway through it, Joel started telling a different story and everybody turned to him.

Julie finished telling the story, mainly just mumbling it to me, since everybody else was listening to Joel.

Steve set up his new plant today.

He put it by the window so it could get enough sunlight.

We sat around and didn't say much about it.

Then Steve said, "Isn't this place, like, a hundred times more cheery?"

Today I worked eight hours at the copy store.

I was tired and looking forward to going home, plopping on my bed and reading more of Watership Down.

When I was unlocking my door I heard paper rustling inside.

I opened the door and saw that Mr. Peterson had strewn all the pages of Watership Down across the floor.

Today Hal made Dan and me scrub the lighted sign above the front door of the copy store.

We found a bird's nest up there.

Dan said, "It looks as though it's been abandoned for some time."

So he tossed it onto the sidewalk and it crumbled into bits.

Today Ruth and I went over to Steve's place.

She saw his new plant and said, "Oh, look, you got a plant."

Then she went off about how to water it, take care of it and everything.

Steve said, "Knowing me, it'll probably just die."

Today I was sitting at the table eating a sandwich.

Mr. Peterson jumped up on the table, looked at me, then walked up on my shoulders.

She got comfortable and just sat there for a while.

when I was done eating and started getting up, she jumped off and ran into the other room.

Today Tony said, "Six full glasses of water per day."

He said that's how much everybody is supposed to drink.

He filled up a glass, drank it, and said, "Delicious."

He set the glass down firmly and said, "That's number three."

Today Ruth and I went to a classical music recital.

The program said the were playing Brahms.

Ruth whispered, "I think it's important to expose yourself to culture, don't you?"

Then she started giggling at the conductor because he was flapping his arms like a lunatic.

Today Steve came over and sat in my chair.

I asked what he was up to and he just said, "Eh."

He said he was feeling kind of gloomy for no particular reason.

"Not enough water," Tony said.

I took Mr. Peterson outside today.

I scooped up some snow and showed it to her and she was afraid of it.

But after a while she was lying belly-up and feeling right at home.

When I brought her back inside, she was wide-eyed, darting back and forth, then stopping suddenly like she was possessed.

Today when I came home I saw the mailman putting mail in the apartment's mail boxes.

I stood there and waited for my mail.

He asked if I was expecting something important today and I said not really.

Today Tony told me the best way to get six glasses of water a day.

"Just always have a glass in your hand, and sip it throughout the day," he said

"Much better than chugging six entire glasses," he said. "Classier, too."

After he left, I noticed that he left his glass on top of my TV.

Ruth came over today.

Tony came by too, and told Ruth, "Are you getting your six glasses a day?"

Ruth smiled and said, "That's what they say, isn't it?"

Then she told Tony that tap water is fluoridated, which she knows because she's a dentist's assistant.

I went to the bookstore today to buy Watership Down.

(Steve loaned me a copy, but it was so worn out it fell apart.)

(And I got caught up in the story so I decided I should buy my own copy.)

I picked it off the shelf and a guy standing there said, "Rabbit book. Cool book."

Today I went to the video store with Ruth.

We didn't know what movie to rent, so we were looking around, trying to find one.

Every movie I wanted to get, Ruth wasn't interested in, and vice versa.

Eventually, we decided not to get anything, and went home.

Today Tony said to me, "Did you know fluoride is poisonous — and it's in our water!?"

I told him I guess I'd heard that.

"Why didn't you stop me when you saw me drinking it all the time?" he asked.

I said I didn't know and he pointed to me and said, "You'll stop at nothing to see me die."

Steve came over today.

He saw Watership Down sitting by my chair and said, "Hey, how do you like it?"

I told him I thought it was pretty good, and that the pages were falling out.

He sat down hard, exhaled loudly and said, out of the blue, "Wouldn't it be great to be, like, Eddie Murphy or somebody?"

Today Tony was making a hamburger and whistling a tune.

"Nothing like a whistled ditty to brighten your day," he said.

I told him that I've never been able to whistle.

"You freak!" he said.

Today Tony told Steve that I couldn't whistle.

Without responding, Steve put his fingers in his mouth and whistled really loud.

Then Tony did the same thing.

Today I was sitting around, trying to whistle.

I've never really been able to, so I was mostly just blowing out air.

But then a loud tooting sound came out, and Mr. Peterson jumped about two feet off the floor.

Then she looked at me like I was crazy.

I decided to make Mr. Peterson a toy out of paper, which she likes to play with.

I crumpled up a piece of paper and tied it to some string.

Mr. Peterson seemed to like it, jumping up at it when I whipped it around.

Also today I worked the evening shift at the copy store and hardly anybody came in.

Today Mr. Peterson was grabbing at my shoelaces while I was walking.

I figured she wanted to play, so I got out her paper-on-a-string toy that I made.

She batted around at it for quite a while, then she got tired of it.

Later, I saw her flipped over by my shoes, chewing on my shoelaces.

Ruth and I went to a garage sale today.

Ruth saw a Batman necklace and said, "Ha! Look at this."

We didn't end up buying anything.

As we left, Ruth said, "There were some neat little things there."

I went for a walk today and saw a dog.

For no reason, she came up to me and barked at me like crazy.

I wondered if there was something wrong with me that the dog could sense.

But after the dog left I realized I was probably okay.

Ruth wanted to go to Steve's today to look at his plant.

"Oh, it's dying," she said.

"I knew it would die," Steve said. "I have no luck with plants."

Ruth tried to think of a way to save it, but couldn't think of anything.

Today I got some stamps.

I got the kind with "love" written on them with the picture of the puppy.

The postal worker gave them to me and smiled.

"Those stamps are cute, aren't they," he said.

Today I was sitting around reading.

I noticed Mr. Peterson sprawled out on the floor, bellied-up.

She occasionally licked her hand, but pretty much stayed in the up-side-down position.

Then suddenly she jumped up and ran in the other room.

Today I was walking around and saw a penny.

I just walked past it without picking it up.

Afterwards I was thinking it was weird to just pass up free money, even if it's just a penny.

Today Hal asked me to work some extra hours next week.

I didn't really feel like it, but I said I would.

"Great," he said.

I'm not sure why I agreed to do it.

I had to get out my winter jacket today.

In a pocket I found an old grocery list.

one of the things on the list was horseradish sauce.

horseradish sauce
chips
cheese
cereal

I couldn't remember ever needing horseradish sauce.

I was scratching Mr. Peterson's head today.

She liked it so much that she kept leaning back.

Finally, she fell over backwards.

Today Ruth came over with a bunch of leaves.

"I want to put them in a book," she said.

She said she used to like doing that when she was a little kid.

So she got wax paper and pressed the leaves and put them in a book and everything.

Tony called me really early this morning.

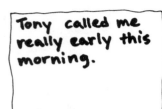

"Jim," he said. "My power went off! What time is it?"

I told him it was 5:30.

He thanked me and hung up.

Tony came by today to look through any newspapers I had.

"I'm cutting out coupons," he said. "Or should I say 'free money.'"

He told me he's already saved almost 3 dollars.

"It's all part of my goal to become a smart shopper," he said.

Ruth and I went to a coffeehouse she found today. 	"Isn't this just the greatest place?" she said. 	I thought it was okay. 	"I think it's just great," she said. 
I woke up this morning hungry for macaroni and cheese. 	I thought about it all day at the copy store. 	On my way home I bought some. 	I cooked it and ate it and I think I waited too long because it didn't taste as good as I'd hoped. 

Today Tony ran up to me and said, "Look what I got in the mail today!"

It was a little coupon book.

He stood there flipping through it for a second.

Then he asked if I'd gotten one in my mail and if he could have it.

Today at the copy store things were pretty slow.

Then for some reason a whole bunch of customers came in.

I worked really fast making all the copies.

After a while everything slowed down again.

Tony came over today, just as Ruth was leaving.

"Hi, Tony!" she said.

After she left, me and Tony just stood there.

Then Tony said, "why is she so damned happy all the time?"

Steve came over today.

He was holding his dead plant.

"I brought a toy for Mr. Peterson," he said.

He put it on the floor and Mr. Peterson sniffed it then walked away.

Today I worked the cash register at the copy store.

It was pretty busy.

After a while I ran out of one-dollar bills.

I told Hal and he said, "You need singles, huh?"

Today I was washing dishes.

Mr. Peterson was standing on the counter, watching.

When a little soap bubble floated past her, she just looked at it.

When it landed on the counter she watched it vanish then put her paw right on the spot where it landed.

Today I went to Ruth's to watch TV and eat popcorn.

The doorbell rang and Ruth said, "Who could that be?"

She got up to see who it was.

It was her friend, and they stood there and talked for half an hour.

Today at the copy store Hal interviewed somebody for a job.

Julie and I were working the counter.

"Another lamb to the slaughter," Julie said.

Then a customer walked up and she said, "May I help you?"

I went to the grocery store today to buy some cereal.

Tony came with.

As I was paying for my cereal, Tony lowered his head and exhaled.

Outside the store he said, "Jim, why didn't you tell me! I have a coupon for that cereal at home for a dollar off!"

Today Hal introduced me to a new employee.

"Her name is Erma," he said.

Then he took her around to see the rest of the store.

She pretty much just followed Hal around and didn't say much.

Today at the copy store Erma was making copies.

"You're getting the hang of things real quick," Hal told her.

Julie commented that Erma doesn't talk much.

"Hey, she's new," Hal said. "She'll loosen up in no time."

Today I was washing dishes.

Mr. Peterson was sitting on the counter, watching.

At one point she reached out her arm and tried to grab a plate I was holding.

I noticed it had some cheese residue on it.

Today at the copy store Erma couldn't figure out something on the big copier.

Dan helped her.

Then he came up to me at the counter.

"Which do you think is the best Twilight Zone episode ever?" he asked.

I went walking around with Tony today.

We stopped at the store to get a snack.

Tony said, "I think I have a coupon for oreos," and started digging through the coupons in his pocket.

Two guys in line behind us started to snicker.

Today when I came home I noticed Mr. Peterson was in the kitchen sink.

As soon as I spotted her she jumped out and ran away.

I looked in there and found a plate that she'd licked clean.

I looked in the other room and saw her licking her hand and rubbing her face.

Tony came over today.

I thought he'd be looking for more coupons, but he wasn't.

"Coupons are dumb," he said.

He turned on the TV and flipped through the channels.

I walked over to Steve's today.

His place was filled with boxes of envelopes and paper.

"I'm helping my mom do some sort of mailing," he said.

We sat around for a while and stuffed envelopes.

I went over to Steve's again today.

"We only have 7000 more envelopes to stuff," he said.

We stuffed envelopes for a while, then played a game on his computer.

"I don't mind taking a lot of breaks," Steve said, "especially since my mom doesn't have any deadline or anything."

Today Ruth told me there was an old house she knew of that looks like a castle.

She took me to go see it.

When we got there it was dark and no lights were on in the house.

"Ooh, scary," she said.

When I came home today Mr Peterson was pacing by the door with her tail sticking up.

I patted her on the head and she rubbed up against my leg.

I sat down and relaxed and she ran back and forth across the apartment.

Today Tony and I stopped at a store for a candy bar.

Tony bought his candy bar and put a penny in the little penny box.

"Here's a little something for you," he told the cashier.

The cashier acted like he didn't even know Tony was there.

Today Steve and I walked by the part of the lake where people ice skate.

"Can you ice skate, Jim?" he asked.

I said I could, but wasn't very good at it or anything.

Steve said he hates all winter sports because they make your feet freeze off.

Tony came over today.

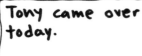

He opened the fridge to look for something to eat.

(He found a can of Pepsi.)

He sat down and said "I think you'd better check your fridge, Jim."

"It smells like something died in there."

Today I looked in my fridge to see if I could find what Tony smelled.

I could sort of smell it, but it wasn't very strong.

I looked way in back and found a leftover container of something I'd forgotten about.

I just threw away the food, the container, and everything.

Ruth came over today.

She brought a present.

At first I thought it was for me, but she said, "It's for Mr. Peterson."

"It's a cat hair brush," she said.

I ran into Mike today.

I used to work with him at McDonald's.

He said he was a stand-up comedian now.

He said he hates when he tells people that because "they always say, 'oh, tell me a joke!'"

Yesterday Ruth told me that it's a good idea to brush cats.

That's why she got me a brush for Mr. Peterson.

I brushed her and she flipped over and exposed her belly.

When I was done she followed me around.

Today Steve and I saw a movie.

When it was over I got up to leave.

But Steve didn't get up, so I sat back down.

(Steve likes to stay for the credits.)

Today I went to buy some soap, then went to work at the copy store.	Dan was working there too. 	I realized I hadn't worked with Dan in quite a while.	Just as I was thinking that he said, "I haven't worked with you in quite a while, Jim."
Steve came over today. 	I told him I ran into Mike and that he's a stand-up comedian now. 	"Everybody's a stand-up comedian now," Steve said. 	"Hey—new soap!" he said. 

Today Steve and I went to see Mike perform his stand-up routine.

It was a small club, and there were hardly any people there.

Mike was the third or fourth comedian to perform, and Steve and I thought he was pretty funny.

He came to sit with us afterwards and said, "Not exactly the Tonight show, but hey."

Today Tony was telling me how cold his feet were.

I noticed he was barefoot, so I suggested he get some slippers.

"Slippers are for sissies," he said.

But he eventually decided slippers weren't such a bad idea.

I washed a load of clothes today.

I sat around and waited while they were in the dryer.

When the machine was done, I checked the clothes and noticed my big towel was still a little damp.

So I ran the dryer a little bit longer.

Today I went to Tony's place.

He was watching a nature documentary on TV.

I thought maybe he was just flipping around the channels, but he wasn't.

After a while he said, "Penguins are amazing!"

We got a fancy new color copier at the copy store today.

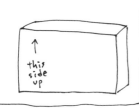

Hal helped the delivery people set it up.

Julie added color copies to our price sign.

"It's the dawning of a new era," Hal said.

Today I was sitting around with Steve when we heard a knock on the door.

It was Tony, and he was wearing big silly moose slippers.

Steve laughed out loud, but Tony wasn't laughing.

"I told my mom I needed some slippers," he said, "and look what she sent me!"

Today Tony called and said I had to come over right away.

So I did.

When I got there, Tony said, "Close your eyes, I've got a surprise."

While my eyes were closed I heard a dog panting and barking.

"You were supposed to be quiet you mutt!" he said. Then he told me the dog was the surprise.

Today Tony told me he was taking care of his brother's dog while he was away.

"He went to Canada," he said.

Tony was throwing around a little bone for the dog.

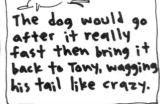

The dog would go after it really fast then bring it back to Tony, wagging his tail like crazy.

"Dogs are great," Tony said.

Today Steve and I went over to see Tony's dog and Steve asked, "What's his name?"

Tony told us his name was "Dog" and showed us how he fetches.

Dog ran after his bone into the other room, and we heard something big fall over and break.

"Dog, no!" Tony yelled.

I usually feed Mr. Peterson first thing in the morning.

But today when I got up I noticed I was out of cat food.

So I had to walk to the store and get some.

By the time I got back it seemed like Mr. Peterson wasn't interested in eating anymore.

Today at the copy store Dan came up to me in the back room.

He said he wanted my advice on something.

"How should I begin a courtship of someone?" he asked.

I told him I didn't have any idea.

Today Tony came by with his dog.

"I thought I'd introduce Dog to Mr. Peterson," he said.

We looked for Mr. Peterson but couldn't find her.

Eventually we noticed she was hiding under the bed.

Last night I was sitting in bed reading my book.

Suddenly I felt like I was flying.

I stopped reading the book so I could feel the sensation better.

Then it stopped, and I went back to reading my book.

Today Ruth and I were out walking when we ran into Tony.

Ruth said, "Oh, look at the cute puppy!" and pet him.

Tony said, "Having a dog is a pain."

"You have to walk the damned things constantly," he said.

Tony's brother came back from his trip today.

So Tony gave him his dog back.

(Tony was taking care of the dog while his brother was away.)

"Having a dog is a hassle," he said. "What I really want is my own children."

At the copy store today Dan was carefully examining two sheets of paper.

He said one was twenty-pound stock and the other was sixty pound.

"I'm trying to figure out exactly what makes them different," he said.

Then Hal came out from the back and yelled, "Get the hell back to work!"

Today when I got up Mr. Peterson was standing on my chest, looking right at me.

As soon as I opened my eyes she let out a big meow and ran into the kitchen.

(That's because she knows she gets fed when I get up.)

After I fed her I looked out the window and saw that it was raining really hard.

Today I accidentally broke a bowl.

It smashed against the sink as I was washing it.

It was a ceramic bowl that was microwave-safe and it was the only one I had.

Little slivers of it flew everywhere and I tried to pick up every last one of them.

Today I went to the store to buy a bowl.

I picked one out and asked the cashier if it was microwave-safe.

She said it should say on the bottom, then tittered and said, "oh—our price tag covers it up!"

So she took a few seconds to pick off the price tag, which was the kind that doesn't come off very easily.

Today I was walking down the street when I saw a guy fixing his bike.

"Hey, could you gimme a hand here?" he said.

I held a wrench while he tightened a screw.

He thanked me, then described how he almost got in an accident a few minutes ago, which is why he stopped to look over his bike.

Today Steve told me he was going to be on the local TV news.

He said he was shopping at the grocery store when the news crew was asking people questions.

I asked him what for and he said they just wanted his opinion about some food-related news story.

"But that doesn't matter," he said. "What matters is I'm gonna be on TV."

Steve was on the local TV news today and we all went to his place to watch.

They did a few national news stories, then they did the story Steve was in.

He was in the grocery store and they asked what he thought about a certain issue and he gave his opinion.

Steve, local resident

We all clapped and cheered, and Steve bowed. Tony said, "You were hardly on two seconds!"

| Today I got up and fed Mr. Peterson.  | when she was done eating she started washing her head.  | She licked her hand then rubbed it on the side of her face a few times. | One time she caused her ear to flip inside-out, and it stayed that way until she rubbed it again and it popped back to its normal position. |
| Today I was calling somebody when Mr. Peterson jumped up on the counter.  | She walked right in front of the phone, so I couldn't dial the number.  | I paused while waiting for her to move, but she just stood there looking at me.  | I put her on the floor and started dialing again, but she jumped up and stood in the same place.  |

Today Tony told me to watch the local news tonight because he was on it.

"I was right on camera, Jim—right on camera," he said.

He said he was walking by the lake when they were doing a story on it or something.

I watched the channel he told me to watch, but I didn't see him on it.

I saw Tony today and told him I watched for him on the news last night but didn't see him.

"Yeah I know," he said. "They must have cut me out."

"'cause I was right on camera, Jim—right on camera."

Then he said, "I guess my public will have to wait for my next big appearance."

Today I came home from work around 9 p.m.

I hung my coat on the door knob without paying attention and it fell on the floor.

I ate, then watched TV for a couple of hours.

I walked past my coat and saw Mr. Peterson sound asleep on it.

I was sitting around today when I thought cookies would taste really good.

So I went to the store to buy some.

The kind I normally get, Keebler Soft Batch chocolate-chip, were sold out, so I settled for chocolate-chip walnut.

They weren't so bad.

Today I came home and hung my coat on the door knob.

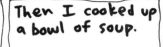

Then I cooked up a bowl of soup.

I heard a repetitive scraping sound coming from the front door, then it stopped.

I went to see what it was and saw Mr. Peterson lying on my coat, which I guess she yanked off the door knob.

Today I was looking out my window.

I was just passing the time.

I would pick a certain person and follow them as long as I could see them.

One person came from inside a building next to mine, then kept walking up the street until all I could see was a speck.

I went over to Ruth's place today.	She was just sitting around reading a book.	I asked her what book she was reading and she told me.	Then she got into explaining the plot and I wasn't interested anymore.
		 (It was a mystery novel)	

I went outside to read my book today.	But it was too cold to be reading outside, so I came back home.	Once I got home, I didn't feel like reading anymore.	And there was nothing on TV either.

I was sitting around today watching TV.	Suddenly I remembered I was supposed to work at the copy store.	I hurriedly grabbed my coat, but I didn't notice Mr. Peterson fast asleep on it.	She got flipped, landed on her side, and ran into the other room.

I brushed my teeth this morning, like any morning.	First, I squeezed some toothpaste onto my brush.	Then, before I got any further, my toothpaste fell off my brush into the sink.	So I squeezed on some more.

Today when I was walking home from the copy store I saw a baby mouse in an alley.

He was sitting in the middle of the alley like he didn't have the sense to hide.

He was really young. It looked like his eyes weren't even open yet.

I could see his little ribs expand as he breathed.

On my way to the copy store today I went through the alley.

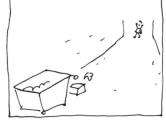

The baby mouse was still there and I leaned in to get a closer look at him.

He must have heard me because he hobbled as fast as he could about five feet, then stopped to catch his breath.

I got some bread crumbs and put them next to him, but he didn't eat them.

Today I was lying in bed trying to fall asleep.

I kept thinking about the baby mouse, wondering why he got abandoned and whether he'd make it.

Mr. Peterson was sitting on the window sill, then suddenly whipped around, trying to catch her tail.

I knew that if Mr. Peterson saw that baby mouse she'd bat him around until he was dead.

On my way to the copy store today I stopped by the alley to see the baby mouse.

He was out in the open, in the middle of the alley.

When I got closer, I could see that he was dead, just lying there, bellied-up.

When I came into the copy store, Joel and everybody were laughing at a joke, but I couldn't help feeling sorry for that mouse.

Today Ruth told me her brother was getting married.

She said she's supposed to be a bridesmaid in the wedding.

"I love weddings," she said, "except when I'm in 'em."

She asked if I wanted to come and I said okay.

Today Ruth took me out to buy a suit for her brother's wedding.

I tried on some suits and felt pretty awkward wearing them.

We eventually picked one, even though I felt just as awkward in it as all the others.

The clerk helping us said to me, "You don't dress up much, do you?" and I said no.

Today Ruth and I drove to her brother's wedding.	We got there and Ruth hugged all her relatives while I just stood there.	The ceremony was quick, and I think I noticed Ruth holding back a tear.	At the reception afterwards a guy said to me, "I give 'em two years tops."

Today there was a knock on my door.	I said, "come in," but nobody came in.	I opened the door and saw Tony on crutches.	"Behold the gimp!" he said.
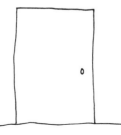	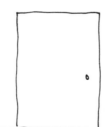		

Yesterday Tony came by on crutches.

He told me he tore some ligaments in his ankle trying to dunk a basketball.

Today he asked me to fix him a bucket of ice because he couldn't carry it in his condition.

He stuck his foot in the ice and winced. Then he said, "Now can you bring me a sandwich?"

Today I was sitting around at home when Tony called.

I went to his place and he asked me to make him some food.

"It hurts just to stand up, Jim, I swear," he said.

I made him a sandwich and while he ate it he said, "My compliments, Jim. The perfect amount of Miracle Whip."

I went over to Mike's today to see what he was up to.

He was sitting with a cast on his leg and with crutches next to him.

He said in a silly dramatic voice, "leave me—I cannot face you as half a man!"

Then he said he was just kidding and to just come right in.

I told Steve today that both Tony and Mike hurt themselves and were on crutches.

We couldn't believe the coincidence.

"Just watch," he said. "Next, I'll break a leg, or you will."

I said yeah and laughed along with him, even though I didn't really think that would happen.

I was walking around outside with Steve today.

we passed by some people juggling on the grass.

we sat and watched them for a while.

"They're pretty good," steve said.

Steve and Ruth came over today to watch a movie on cable.

It was Under Siege.

We watched it and ate popcorn that Ruth brought.

When it was over we turned off the TV, sat around and didn't say much of anything.

Today Mike and I were hanging out together.

Mike had to go to the comedy club tonight and he was thinking up new material.

"I'm actually glad this happened to my knee," he said. "because now I can joke about it."

"For once I can stop using the silly fat-guy gimmick," he said.

Today Mike came over and we just sat around.

As he was leaving Tony came over.

They had trouble maneuvering through the door with their crutches.

We all thought it was kind of funny.

I went over to Steve's place today.

"Watch this, Jim," he said. "watch this."

Then he juggled for about two seconds until he lost control of all the balls.

"Pretty good, huh?" he said.

Today Tony came over on his crutches.

He set them by the door and said, "check this out," Jim.

He took a few cautious steps, yelling, "It's a miracle! It's a miracle!"

(He explained that part of his rehabilitation was to walk and stuff.)

Ruth and I went to see Mike perform at the comedy club today.

He made up a funny story about how he broke his knee fighting Black Belt Jones.

(He actually fell over a guard rail in the parking lot.)

When he was done he sat with us and Ruth said to me, "Isn't it neat that we know someone famous?"

Today Ruth and I went to see her friend Susan.

She had just had a baby, which she named Alice, and we held her.

She was very small.

"She's so small," Ruth said.

Today I got up early.	I worked at the copy store from 10 a.m. till 4 p.m.	I worked with Joel, who at one point said, "This place is nowhere, man."	Then I went home and Mr. Peterson, who was napping on the chair arm, looked up at me for a second or two, then went back to sleep.

I called some company today and they put me on hold for a long time.	I just sat there and listened to the Muzak.	I heard renditions of "You Are So Beautiful," and a Billy Joel song that I don't know the name of.	When the next available representative finally answered, I forgot all about the music.

| when I got up today the floor was cold.  | So I put on some socks.  | Later in the day I told Tony about the cold floor.  | He gave me the pair of silly moose slippers his mom gave him.  |

| Today when I got up the floor was cold.  | I put on Tony's silly moose slippers.  | They were warm.  | As I walked, Mr. Peterson batted at the little foam antlers that stick out.  |

Today after I got up I ate a bowl of cereal.

I didn't have anything to read or look at while I ate, so I stared at the cereal box.

In small printing on the side of the box was a toll-free number I could call if I had any questions about the cereal.

I stared at it during almost the entire time I ate and couldn't think of any questions I would ask.

Today I got up a little late, and was supposed to work at the copy store.

I fed Mr. Peterson.

Then I ate a banana and an english muffin while getting dressed.

I got outside and was surprised to see that it had snowed quite a bit.

Today I went to Ruth's place and she answered the door slumped over in her bath robe.

"I have a cold," she said.

She also said she didn't know if it would be a good idea to visit her.

"You don't want this cold," she said.

Today Ruth called me and asked if I'd pick up some cold medicine for her.

I said I would and headed out to the store.

They didn't have the kind she wanted, so I got a different brand.

I showed up at her place and explained that they were out of the kind she wanted and she said, "whatever."

| Today Ruth was telling me about a bad dream she had.  | She was working at the dentist's office, like she normally does.  | Except her dentist was Frankenstein's monster.  | "It was so scary I woke up in the middle of the night screaming," she said.  |

| Ruth is finally getting over her cold.  | "I'm so happy it's over with," she said.  | Then she noticed that she was all out of Kleenexes.  | She flattened the box and put it in the trash.  |

Today I was walking home from work after dark.

I noticed it was a clear night and you could see all the stars.

I decided to lie in the snow and stare up at the sky for a while.

I started to get sleepy and felt like I didn't have the energy to get up.

Ruth said today that my apartment could use some cleaning.

"I don't mean to sound rude," she said, "but men are slobs."

She said she'd help me clean, and that it would be no big deal.

We started by vacuuming and dusting. (Ruth vacuumed and I dusted.)

I finished cleaning my apartment today.

I scrubbed the bathroom and the kitchen and everything.

I even scrubbed out the kitchen cabinets.

When I was done, I had a lot of energy left, but I took a nap anyway.

Today was trash day.

I got out a big plastic garbage bag to fill it with all my trash.

I tried to open it, but it wouldn't open.

I realized I was trying to open the wrong end, so I tried the other end and it opened right up.

Today I went to the grocery store to buy a whole bunch of food.

I got milk, bread, frozen peas, apples, hot dogs and some macaroni & cheese.

While I put all the food away, Mr. Peterson jumped in the bag and stayed there for a long time.

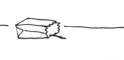

I cooked up some macaroni & cheese with chopped-up hot dogs in it and watched TV.

Today I was just sitting around watching TV.

Tony came over and said, "Hey, Jim, how's it goin'?"

We sat and watched TV for a while.

He started sniffing and said, "Did you clean or something?"

Ruth came over to visit today.

We were just sitting around when we noticed Mr. Peterson sneezing.

Ruth reached out to her and said, "God bless you, Mr. Peterson."

Mr. Peterson ran away as fast as she could.

Steve and I were walking around today when we heard a funny squeaking noise.

It was coming from a squirrel who was sitting next to a dumpster.

We noticed he was looking up at another squirrel who was eating an english muffin wrapper.

Steve said, "It would appear the one below wants the other one's english muffin wrapper."

It was really cold outside today.

I stayed inside and read a book.

Mr. Peterson sat right under my light, so I couldn't see.

I moved her out of the way and she squawked at me and went right back under the light.

Today Ruth and I went out to eat.

"This place is pretty good," she said.

I went into the bathroom, where somebody had etched something on the wall.

"This place sucks!" it said.

Today Tony popped his head in the door.

He said, "Jim!" Then he said "Wait, hold on."

Then he was talking to somebody in the hall.

Then he just closed the door and didn't come back.

Today I was planning to do my laundry.

But I noticed I didn't have any quarters.

I went to the bank to get some.

The teller gave me the quarters and said, "Doin' laundry?"

Tony came over today.

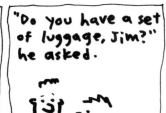

"Do you have a set of luggage, Jim?" he asked.

I said not really.

"I should get me one," he said.

Today as I was leaving my apartment I noticed a cat in the hall.

Before I knew it Mr. Peterson bolted out the door toward the other cat.

They just stood in front of each other for a second.

Then the other one hissed and Mr. Peterson hightailed it back inside.

Today I went to the store with Tony to buy some luggage.

"I think everybody should own a quality set of luggage," he said.

The salesperson showed us the lowest-priced set, which cost $500, and Tony said, "Alright, thanks anyway."

As we were leaving, Tony said, "Can you believe that place? 500 bucks for suitcases!"

Today after working at the copy store I came home and sat down.

Mr. Peterson came out of the bedroom, groggy-looking.

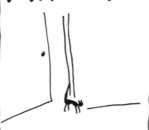

She did a big stretch, then walked over to me.

She jumped on my lap and folded her hands in.

Today Steve and I went bowling.

We were no good at it, so we didn't play for very long.

As we were handing in our shoes, Steve told me he was going on a trip.

I asked him where and he said, "To visit my grandparents. wanna come with?"

Today Steve and I drove to the small town where his grandparents live.

We stopped at a gas station on the highway.

We looked over the food and stuff to get something for the road.

"Not the best selection of snack cakes I've ever seen," Steve said.

Steve and I arrived at his grandparents' house today.

Steve's grandma said, "Oh good. Two strong boys. I could use some help in the yard."

So we spent the day hauling some bricks in her back yard.

Steve's grandpa woke up from a nap, came outside and said, "Is that young Steve?"

Today Steve and I explored the town where his grandparents live.

It's pretty small— only about one thousand people, Steve's grandpa said.

We went down to the pond by their house and saw a white rabbit.

We went to a Dairy Queen-type place and the guy said, "You in town for the Polka Fest?"

Today Steve and I helped his grandpa down in his basement workshop.

He was sawing up wood to build a bird house.

He held up a piece and said, "Look at that wood. Only the good lord can make something so beautiful."

My job was to grab the scrap wood off the table saw and throw it in the bin.

Today I got up and ate some pancakes that Steve's grandma made.

She patted his grandpa and said, "Grandpa just loves his pancakes."

After we ate, we hung up Grandpa's birdhouse and sat on the porch.

"I think that house will be a big hit in the spring." Steve's grandma said.

Steve and I drove back home today.

While we were driving, we saw a sign that said, "Treever, population 140."

Steve said, "Hey, let's get jobs at the cafe in Treever and live there."

He sort of chuckled then said, "Could you imagine that?"

When I got home yesterday, Mr. Peterson was eating a kleenex.

I took it away from her and she ran around the apartment for a while.

Ruth, who took care of Mr. Peterson while I was gone, left a note.

It had an account of the past few days' events, and said, "I think Mr. Peterson misses you!"

Today I got a bunch of junk mail.

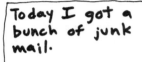

I threw it on the floor and Mr. Peterson tried to burrow in it.

But she got tired of it after a while.

Today Ruth and I played a game of miniature Battleship.

(Her sister got it for her as a gift.)

At the end of the game I located her biggest ship.

When I did, she said, "You sunk my battleship!" and laughed.

Today was a pretty cold day.

I came inside and took off my coat and grabbed a kleenex.

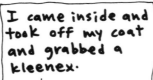

A new kleenex automatically popped out of the box when I grabbed one.

I examined the box to see if I could figure out how it worked.

Today I was just lying around doing nothing.

Then Steve called and said he'd be right over with some incredible news.

Before he came over, I fixed myself a sandwich and ate it.

He came over and told me he was the lucky winner of a ten dollar shopping spree at the grocery store.

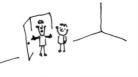

Today I went with Steve to help spend his ten dollar shopping spree.

He was explaining how he registered for it by dropping his name in a box at the store.

"I used to think nobody ever won those things," he said.

We arrived at the store and they didn't even give him a shopping spree. They just handed him a ten dollar bill.

I worked at the copy store today.

Julie told me that today was her birthday.

I wished her a happy birthday.

"Oh, shut up," she said.

Today at the copy store, Steve came in.

He asked if he could use the self-serve copier and I said sure.

After he made his copies, he came back to the checkout counter.

He asked me, "How can you stand working here?"

I went to the store with Tony today.

We were looking at the magazine rack.

"I should subscribe to more magazines," he said. "You know, to keep informed."

Then he picked up some tattoo-biker magazine and said, "You should get this one, Jim."

Today Tony was reading Rolling Stone magazine, which he bought the other day.

"You'll never guess how much Janet Jackson makes in a year," he said.

I said I didn't have any idea.

"A lot," he said.

Tony came over today and said, "I've decided how I'm gonna make my millions, Jim."

"Writing songs!" he shouted.

He said big-name recording artists are always looking for good new material.

Then he asked if I had any ideas for a song.

Last night I was sitting in bed staring at the ceiling.

I wasn't tired, so I just sat there.

I felt Mr. Peterson jump up on the bed and walk up my legs.

Then she came up to my face and I could feel her cold, wet nose touch my face.

Today some people were painting the inside of Ruth's apartment.

Ruth made polite conversation with the painters, but they didn't seem to want to talk.

They brought a radio, which they had tuned to the rock station.

So Ruth decided we should leave them alone, and we walked around outside even though it was kind of cold.

Today Ruth and I went to Steve's place.

Ruth's apartment was still being painted, and she just needed some place to go.

We played some of Steve's computer games.

Ruth played along and had a good time even though she kept saying she was no good at video games.

Ruth and I watched the local TV news for a while today.

Mr. Peterson was trying to burrow into Ruth's new coat, which was on the big chair.

A report on the news told about somebody who got shot.

Ruth said, "Wouldn't it just be terrible to be shot?"

Today Mr. Peterson was sleeping on top of my backpack, which was on top of the table.

I didn't notice at first, but she was pretty far off the edge of the table.

Suddenly the backpack fell and Mr. Peterson fell off the table with it.

She ran across the room and shook her head so hard I could hear her ears flapping.

Today at the copy store Julie was carrying a big box of paper.

She had to walk through the narrow passage where I was standing.

So she headed straight for me and said, "Move. Move. Move."

I got out of the way and she walked right by.

Today Steve and I were watching TV.

We watched the Star Trek episode where Data learns to be funny.

When it was over, Steve asked me, "Jim, do you think I'm a funny guy?"

I said I guess so.

Today Steve told me he's been talking to Mike about working together.

He said they thought of a funny TV sitcom idea.

"It would be set in Hell," he said.

He said they were thinking of writing a script for the pilot episode.

Today Steve and I went over to Mike's.

They were planning to write a TV sitcom that takes place in Hell.

"Hey," Mike said, "Let's call it 'Hell in a Handbasket.'"

Steve laughed and said, "Perfect!"

I went over to Mike's place today.

He and Steve were there to write a TV script.

But we mostly just sat around talking.

"What I'd really like to write is a super-hero movie," Steve said.

I ran into Steve today.

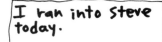

I asked him how his TV script writing was coming along.

"I don't know," he said, "we haven't done much on it."

Then he yelled, "Look out!" just as a guy on a bicycle came barreling down the sidewalk.

I ran into Mark today.

He was in creative writing class with me a long time ago.

He asked what was up and I told him a couple of my friends were writing a TV sitcom script.

"TV is a vast wasteland," he said.

I decided to start reading a book today.

It's "The Sirens of Titan," by kurt Vonnegut.

So far, it's a pretty good book.

Tony and I played basketball today.

He knew of a park nearby that had a basketball court.

We didn't play a real game or anything. we just leisurely shot some baskets.

Every time Tony made a basket without hitting the rim, he'd say, "Nuthin' but net!"

Tony and I played basketball again today.

Today we decided to play a game of HORSE.

Tony realized I was no good at lay-ups, so he won by doing a lot of lay-ups.

It started to get dark and he wanted to keep playing but my hands were getting cold.

Mike came over today.

He said he just stopped by because he didn't have anything to do.

Then he saw Mr. Peterson and said he had to go.

(Mike's allergic to cats.)

Today Ruth came home from her job and sighed.

"I really like my job," she said, "but sometimes it's rough."

She explained a complicated story about how a supplier at the dentist's office was causing her budget problems.

She asked, "What do you think I should do?" and I didn't have any idea.

Today at the copy store I noticed Dan and Julie boxing up some copies.

They were playing a game, trying to stuff paper into the box faster than the other person.

It got to where they just crammed it in so fast that the paper got crumpled up and was flying everywhere.

Then they stopped, because they couldn't help but crack up laughing.

Today Ruth and I went to a record store.

Ruth bought a Mariah Carey CD.

"She's such a good singer," she said.

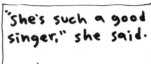

We saw a Red Hot Chili Peppers poster and Ruth said, "My sister looks like them."

Today I was hanging out at Ruth's place.

She told me to stay right where I was, and she went into the other room.

She came out with a camera and said, "Say cheese!"

But the camera didn't click, and she couldn't figure out what was wrong with it.

Steve rented "The Big Picture," which is about making Hollywood movies.

He said he liked it because he could relate to it after dabbling in show business.

Tony said, "The closest you've ever come to show biz is watching Entertainment Tonight."

Steve corrected Tony by explaining that he tried writing a script a while ago.

Today Ruth and I went to a camera repair shop.

camera Repair

Ruth was picking up her camera, which got repaired there.

She said it was no wonder it needed to be fixed, since it had just been sitting around collecting dust for months.

As we were leaving she said, "Now let's go buy some film."

Today at the copy store Dan was making copies.	He asked Joel how many he was supposed to make.	Joel said, "Duh," and pointed to the order slip, which says how many.	He walked away shaking his head.

Today Ruth took my picture.	Later, we went over to Steve's and took his picture.	Steve said to Ruth, "What are you, on vacation?"	She said she was just taking some pictures.

Today at work Dan was working the register.

Joel walked up to him and started talking, but I couldn't hear what they were saying.

But I heard Joel say, "Whatever, you fat little turd," when he walked away.

I noticed Dan had a scowl on his face, and all his skin was redder than usual.

Today during my lunch break at the copy store I was eating at the same time as Joel.

We weren't saying much.

Joel took a Pepsi out of the fridge and opened it.

I told him it was Dan's and he said, "So what?"

Today I worked the afternoon shift at the copy store.

I was working the register when I heard yelling and boxes being thrown in the back room.

Then I saw Dan stomp out of the store, pointing to Joel, saying, "I'm sick of your crap!"

All the customers stared, and Hal, the manager, stood there not saying anything.

I went to see Dan today.

He said, "I wonder if people are mean because of genes or environment."

I said I didn't know.

He said he tends to side with B. F. Skinner on the issue.

Today I came to work and Dan said, "Guess what."

I asked what and he told me that Joel got fired.

"There is justice in the galaxy," he said.

He went about making copies, whistling.

Today I was walking through my apartment and Mr. Peterson was standing directly in my path.

I walked right up to her and she didn't move.

So I stepped over her, one leg to each side of her.

She looked up at me and almost flipped over backwards.

I went to Ruth's place today.

She asked me over to show me something she made.

She said, "Are you ready?" and I said yes.

She turned on the light and there was a mobile hanging from her ceiling with photos of all her friends on it.

Today I decided to go visit my mom back in my hometown.

"Jim! well, hello," she said.

She told me I came just in time because she was cooking a big meal.

I went into the dining room and my grandma said, "Jim! well, hello."

(I didn't know my grandma would be there, too.)

I've been visiting my mom for a while.

Today we drove to my Aunt Harriet and Uncle Gene's farmhouse.

My mom and Aunt Harriet paired off and went to look at the garden.

Uncle Gene said to me, "So I hear you're in the copying business."

Today I went walking around by my mom's house.

Just past her house is open country.

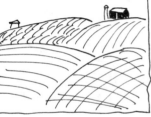

I decided to go into one of the corn fields, even though when I was little grown-ups used to warn against walking in corn fields because it's easy to get lost in there when the stalks are really tall.

But I got out of it just fine.

Today I walked over to Julie's house.

(She was an old friend from high school.)

Her mom remembered me and said, "Oh hi, Jim."

I asked her if Julie was around and she said she hasn't been home in two years.

Today it was kind of gloomy outside so I sat around and watched TV.

There was some kind of stand-up comedian on who was pretty funny.

Then nothing else was on, but I kept watching and flipping channels.

I watched until my eyes hurt.

I went over to my Dad's today.

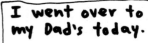

He showed me the deck he's building behind his house.

He said, "I could use some help putting in the last few two-by-sixes."

So we spent the afternoon drilling planks, listening to the hits on his transistor radio.

I came back home today after a week at my mom's.

Mr. Peterson seemed pretty indifferent.

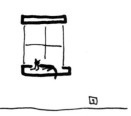

I put my stuff away then sat down and relaxed.

Mr. Peterson rubbed up against my leg once, then went into the other room.

Today Ruth told me she read my journal while I was gone.

She seemed kind of sad, so I asked what was the matter.

"You don't have anything in here about us getting married," she said.

"It's all... little, meaningless stuff," she said.

Today Ruth asked why I only write about little, un-important things in my journal.

I said I didn't know why, but I just end up doing it that way.

She asked if I could at least write in something about our wedding.

I said I would.

Ruth and I got married today.	Ruth was nervous and excited.	All her relatives were there, and so were mine.	Like my mom, dad and grandma, who was wearing a pin shaped like an owl.

Today Ruth and I were just sitting around, not doing much of anything.	Ruth said, "Hey, wouldn't it be fun to drive around the country?"	I said I guess that would be a fun thing to do.	She said, "Yup." and that was all we said about it.

Today Ruth asked me, "So, when should we go on our big cross-country drive?"

I didn't realize she had seriously wanted to go, so I said, "I don't know."

She said she's been saving money from her dental lab job and would like to go right away.

I went to the copy store to tell Hal, and he said, "But Jim, now's when I need you most."

Today I told Tony that Ruth and I were planning to go on a big trip.

"Great," he said. "Just don't tell me any of the mushy details."

He said he's always wanted to go on a cross-country trip.

"Hey, can I come?" he said. "I'll just sit in back and not say anything, I promise."

Today Ruth showed me how much stuff she'd packed in her suitcase and all the routes she drew up on her maps.

She got giddy talking about all the things we could do and the places we could go.

Then I told her that Tony said he wanted to come on our trip with us.

Suddenly, and for the first time I can ever remember, Ruth wasn't smiling.

Today Tony said, "Hey Jim, you knew I was just kidding about coming on that road trip with you, right?"

Then he asked all about the trip. I told him Ruth was hoping to leave right away and be gone a few weeks.

"Jim," he said ominously, "don't you see what's going on with Ruth?"

I said no, and he whispered intensely, "She's running from the law!"

Today Ruth and I left for our big cross-country trip.

We talked for the first few hours and I started to get really tired.

When I woke up it was dark outside.

I asked Ruth where we were and she said, "Princeton, Illinois."

Today Ruth and I drove through St. Louis, Missouri.

We decided it would be fun to go to the top of the arch, so we got off the interstate into downtown.

We eventually figured out how to get to the arch entrance, and managed to find a place to park.

But the arch was closed for the day.

Ruth and I have been eating a lot of Mountain Dew and potato chips.

Today we stopped at a restaurant in Columbia, Missouri.

Ruth said, after a few bites, "This is pretty good food."

But then we decided it was about the same as food anywhere.

Today we drove through Kansas.

We couldn't believe that the landscape never changed, hour after hour.

We stopped so Ruth could take my picture.

Then I took hers.

We drove through Denver today.

Ruth said, "Let's stop and look around, okay?"

So we pulled off the highway, parked, and walked around.

We went into some stores, and Ruth saw a jacket and said, "That's a great-looking jacket."

Today Ruth and I drove most of the day without stopping much.

"Jim," Ruth said, "Did you ever wonder what would've happened if we never met?"

I told her I guess I never did.

Then we got to talking about how we met, working at MacDonald's

We pulled into a truck stop today to fill up the tank and just stop and stretch.

Ruth bought some doughnuts and a funny cap.

We stood in line then paid for our stuff.

The cashier said, "You have a good day now, and may God bless you both."

Today we played the license plate ABC game for a while.

We also passed some mountains that Ruth wanted to stop and look at.

So we did.

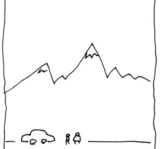

Today we were driving along the highway when a fawn jumped right in front of the car.

Ruth screamed and hit the brakes, but he appeared too suddenly and we ran right over him.

Ruth froze up, and her hands got so shaky she had to pull over.

Then she started sobbing.

Ruth hasn't been talking much.

Today we drove through Las Vegas.

I asked Ruth if she wanted to stop and see anything and she said not unless I did.

I kept driving, and noticed that every sign had fancy blinking lights on it, even the MacDonald's one.

Today Ruth and I drove into Santa Fe, New Mexico.

Ruth bought some jewelry from one of the Indian merchants on the street.

It was a ring, which she put on as soon as she bought it.

She said she couldn't believe all the stuff you could buy here.

Ruth and I have been trading off sleeping and driving.

Today we finally decided that sleeping in the car is uncomfortable.

So we stopped at a camping ground and set up Ruth's tent.

But there were so many mosquitoes and howling coyotes that it was even worse than sleeping in the car.

Today we got to Houston, Texas.

Ruth's high-school friend Tammy lives here, so we stayed at her house.

We sat in her living room and she and Ruth talked about all that's happened since high school.

Tammy had two kids, and one of them kept staring at me.

Today I was woken up by Tammy's kids playing and laughing outside my room.

It was 6am and Tammy was getting ready for work, so Ruth and I had to leave too.

Tammy thanked us for coming, and told me it was very nice meeting me.

Ruth asked what her kids were supposed to do all day and Tammy said, "oh, they'll be fine."

As we drove out of Texas, Ruth told me about her friend Tammy. "It's a sad story," she said.

She told me about how Tammy got married right after high school, then divorced after having two kids.

Then a big truck passed us on the highway and honked at us.

honk honk

Ruth said "oop!" after noticing she was going 45 mph in the fast lane.

Today we went to Graceland.

Elvis's actual mansion was a lot smaller than we thought it would be.

"I feel faint!" a guy in the tour group said. (He was just joking.)

Then we ate in the Hound Dog Cafe, and noticed that there were a lot of flies there.

Today we stopped in Cave City, Kentucky.

Ruth bought a postcard to send to Steve back home.

"What should I say?" she asked me.

I said I don't know, and she stood there staring at the card.

Today we drove up the South Carolina coastline.

We stopped and ate at some beaches along the way.

"This is beautiful," Ruth said.

At one stop we watched some jet fighters put on an air show.

We drove up the east coast more today, through North Carolina and Virginia.

"I just can't believe how beautiful this is," Ruth said.

We stopped at a beach and walked along the surf.

We passed a little kid, playing with an up-turned bucket in the sand, who said, "Don't smash my castle, please."

We went on some of the Washington DC tours today.

We saw the White House, the capitol, and the Washington Monument.

I can't even remember all the things we saw.

After our tours we relaxed by the water and agreed that going on tours is pretty tiring.

Today Ruth and I got to New York City.

In Manhattan, it seemed like we were the only car that wasn't a taxi or limousine.

Ruth was really nervous driving, "because the other cars are so rude," she said.

Along the way, we noticed a funny parking sign.

Today we walked through Central Park.

It was full of a lot of people walking their dogs and their kids' strollers.

We watched the little boats on the pond for a while.

Ruth thought she saw Spike Lee, but couldn't be sure about it.

Today we roamed around New York City some more.

We walked to Times Square.

We also went to the GE Building because Ruth wanted to buy a David Letterman T-shirt while she still could.

Then we went to the Metropolitan Museum and saw some really old mummies.

Today we drove through Connecticut and into Massachusetts.

We drove all the way to the tip of Cape Cod.

There was an artsy fishing village there that we liked.

We stayed there for a while and ate at a restaurant on a pier, and the smell of fish was everywhere.

Today we started to head back home.

We listened to a Best of Elvis Costello tape Ruth got in Boston.

We listened to it over and over until we got sick of it.

When I took over driving, Ruth slept and mumbled something in her sleep that I couldn't make out.

Steve took care of Mr. Peterson while I was away.

"Hey, you'll never guess what Mr. Peterson likes to eat," he said.

I asked him what.

"Corn!" he said.

I went to the copy store today to tell Hal I was back.

"We could sure use you, Jim," he said.

He rubbed his forehead and said, "Things haven't been going so great around here."

Then he smiled and said, "So, how was your big trip?"

Ruth and I went to look at apartments today.

One place didn't allow pets, another was too expensive...

"This apartment hunting is tiring," Ruth commented at one point.

After a long day of looking at apartments, we relaxed at Hardee's and ate shakes.